MA

of North-Western Australia

by Carolyn Thomson-Dans
and Brent Johnson

Department of
Environment and Conservation

INTRODUCTION

The Kimberley region is probably the best place in Western Australia for viewing native mammals in the wild. If you drive out from the main towns you are bound to see agile wallabies. In places such as Geikie Gorge you can see large colonies of roosting flying foxes. If you know where to look, you will be rewarded with more unusual sightings, such as the nocturnal sugar gliders at Mount Hart homestead.

This is because, unlike other parts of WA, the north Kimberley has most of the original mammal species. In the deserts and the south-west numerous species have either completely disappeared, or declined seriously in abundance to the point where they are only found on offshore islands. The mammal fauna in the Kimberley has probably survived intact largely because of the absence of the introduced European fox. Fortunately, the fox cannot survive in the region's warm, tropical climate. There is, however, a new threat to native animals of the north with the invasion of the introduced cane toad. This pest has caused the decline of many species across the top of Australia as it continues its march westward from Queensland. This prolific breeder carries a toxin at all stages of its life cycle that kills the naive native predators.

Wildfires are also a significant threat to the natural cycles that have evolved during Aboriginal occupation of the north. With a disruption to traditional burning regimes, grasses grow unchecked and ultimately ignite in fires that cover huge areas and burn for many weeks. Sensitive habitats suffer from these hot fires and are being replaced by grassland which is less likely to support native mammals.

Although there are marked differences in the mammal fauna from north to south, you can see a similar suite of mammal species. For instance, in the south the chuditch occupies a similar niche to the northern quoll of the Pilbara and Kimberley. There are

Black-footed rock wallaby

different kinds of brushtail possums in the north and the south. The Kimberley still has the northern nailtail wallaby, whereas the crescent nailtail wallaby of southern Australia has not been seen for decades and is presumed extinct. The Kimberley is as close as you will come on the Australian mainland to seeing the complete range of native mammals found before European settlement. Of course, if you are travelling to the Pilbara you will also see an abundance of mammals, including the fruit bats of the oasis at Millstream and the rock wallabies of the Dampier Archipelago and Millstream-Chichester National Park.

ECHIDNA

(Tachyglossus aculeatus)

The echidna is best known for its amazing biology. Like the platypus, this mammal lays eggs and suckles its young. The echidna and platypus are in a primitive group known as monotremes. When disturbed, the echidna either curls into a spiny ball to protect its soft underside, or digs its belly into the soil, so that only the spines are exposed.

DESCRIPTION: Long spines cover the body and fur is present between them. These creatures have a bulbous forehead and a long snout to collect their food. Males have a spur on the ankle of the hindleg but, unlike that of the platypus, this is not venomous.

OTHER NAMES: Spiny anteater.

STATUS AND DISTRIBUTION: Echidnas are widely distributed throughout the Australian continent and Tasmania. Although they are not considered threatened, they are no longer frequently seen on the Australian mainland. However, they may be locally abundant in areas such as the Burrup Peninsula.

PREFERRED HABITAT: They may be found in any place with a good supply of ants and termites.

LIFE HISTORY: Echidnas are usually solitary. However, when they mate between July and August, several males may congregate around a single female. About two weeks later, a single soft-shelled egg is deposited directly into the pouch. This hatches after 10 days and the young remains in the pouch, where it suckles milk exuded from the mother's mammary glands. Here it stays for about three months. Completely hairless when born, the youngsters are covered with short spines by the time they leave the pouch. These toothless animals expose termite galleries by breaking

open nests with their strong forepaws or snout or digging into soil. They then extract the termites with long, sticky tongues. Dingoes and goannas will occasionally eat echidnas. Their relative abundance on large, fox-free islands such as Kangaroo Island in South Australia suggests that the fox is also a significant predator.

HOW TO SEE THEM: Secretive echidnas are rarely seen. However, extensive diggings at the base of termite mounds and along tracks are a sure sign of their presence. If you are bushwalking and notice large excavations under a log, try shining a torch inside it to see if the digger is still around. These mammals have distinctive cylindrical droppings in which ant remains are easily distinguished.

Droppings

NORTHERN QUOLL

(Dasyurus hallucatus)

The northern quoll is smaller, slimmer and more delicately proportioned than its southern cousin, the chuditch. Otherwise, its appearance and life history is similar. Like the chuditch, it has attractive, camouflaging white spots on the brown fur covering its head and upper body, a pointed tapering snout and an aggressive disposition. It often lives in and around dwellings inhabited by people.

DESCRIPTION: This species has the white spotted brown fur characteristic of all quolls. The tail is brown but has no spots. Its underparts are cream to white. Northern quolls also have grooved pads on their hind feet, which may help them to climb on smooth rocky surfaces. They are larger than a rat and adults weigh between 300 and 900 grams, with males far larger and heavier than females.

OTHER NAMES: Little northern native cat, satanellus, north Australian native cat.

STATUS AND DISTRIBUTION: This mammal is found in the Pilbara and Kimberley regions of northern WA and across the rest of northern Australia to Queensland. However, it is absent from the central deserts of these regions. Now regarded as endangered, it has declined from drier parts of its range and in areas occupied by cane toads.

PREFERRED HABITAT: The northern quoll is found largely in broken rocky country sparsely covered by vegetation, such as open forests, savannah and woodland.

LIFE HISTORY: These nocturnal mammals hunt native rodents and small marsupials, birds, reptiles and insects. They supplement this diet with figs and other fruits. By day they sleep in a hollow log or rocky crevice. Northern

quolls spend much of their time on the ground. The males often aggressively defend a home range and its resident females from other males. Females often remain in the place where they were born but most males leave at an early age. The female has no pouch, but they develop enlarged nipples partly surrounded by a flap of skin when in breeding condition. Between one and eight hairless young are born in July. They remain attached to the nipples for eight to 10 weeks. By September, the surviving young will be left in dens and suckled to about five months of age.

WHERE TO SEE THEM: They like to raid rubbish bins at camping sites. Visitors to stations such as Mount Hart, in the Kimberley, may see them in the garden if spotlighting at night. Northern quolls are numerous on Koolan island in the Buccaneer Archipelago.They are also seen on islands off the Burrup Peninsula and at Python Pool in the Millstream–Chichester National Park.

MULGARA

***(Dasycercus* sp.)**

The mulgara was recently divided into two species – the crest-tailed mulgara, (*Dasycercus cristicauda*) and the brush-tailed mulgara, (*Dasycercus blythi*). These muscular carnivorous marsupials are found in Australia's arid centre. They hunt large invertebrates and small animals and can survive on the water they obtain from their food.

DESCRIPTION: Larger than a mouse with a maximum head and body length of 220 millimetres, mulgaras are a light reddish-brown or tan above and whitish below. The tail on crest-tailed mulgaras is short, reddish-brown and flattened at the base and has a distinctive crest of black hairs while brush-tailed mulgaras have much of the tail covered in black hair without a crest and short rounded ears. The ears on crest-tailed mulgaras are larger Males are generally larger than females in both species.

STATUS AND DISTRIBUTION: Mulgaras are known from small, scattered populations in the deserts, including near the Kennedy Range and the Collier Range. They they do not reach the Kimberley region. In WA crest-tailed mulgaras are regarded as a threatened species.

PREFERRED HABITAT: These marsupials inhabit arid sandy regions that support spinifex grasslands.

LIFE HISTORY: Mulgaras dig complex burrows on the flats between sand dunes. They are thought to be quite long-lived, and may survive for six or more years, continuing to grow throughout their life. The females give birth to up to eight young once each year.

WHERE TO SEE THEM: They are not completely nocturnal and are sometimes seen sunbathing near the entrances of their burrows. Visitors to arid areas may have a chance encounter, especially after good rains.

ANTECHINUSES

Four species of antechinus - small carnivorous marsupials that are rarely seen - are found in the Pilbara region of WA. They are the little red antechinus (*Dasykaluta rosamondae*), the fat-tailed antechinus (*Pseudantechinus macdonnellensis*), Rory's pseudantechinus (*Pseudantechinus roryi*) and Woolley's antechinus (*Pseudantechinus woolleyae*). A fifth species, the Ningbing antechinus (*Pseudantechinus ningbing*), is almost confined to the Kimberley.

The little red antechinus lives in a maze of spinifex tussocks. This animal is inquisitive, nocturnal and kills and eats insects, lizards and other small vertebrates. Its head and body is about 10 centimetres long. Its fur is brown with coppery tones and reasonably dense and spiky. The head and ears are fairly short. It is found in the Pilbara and the western Great Sandy Desert and south to the Kennedy Range National Park.

Like many of its close relatives such as phascogales, the males of this species all die soon after the mating season. Mating is an epic affair which lasts for several hours, and the mass deaths are stress-related!

The fat-tailed antechinus lives in rocky hills and breakaways and sometimes within termite mounds. It is greyish-brown and has chestnut patches behind the ears. They sometimes emerge during the day to sunbathe. The species is found across the arid centre, including large areas of WA and the Northern Territory. Fat is stored in the exceptionally stout tail in times of plenty. Each female has a single litter of up to six young in late August or September. Unlike the little red antechinus, the males may survive to breed another year.

Roryi's pseudantechinus is similar to Woolley's pseudantechinus but is smaller with reddish-brown fur and a bi-coloured tail. Little is known of the habits of these two species.

The Ningbing antechinus resembles the fat-tailed antechinus but has a longer tail with very little hair and a scaly appearance. It is light greyish-brown and has chestnut patches behind the ears.

WHERE TO SEE THEM: Sadly, people are most likely to see a dead antechinus brought in by a domestic cat. Unless they pay close attention, these could well be mistaken for house mice.

Above: Little red antechinus

Below: Fat-tailed antechinus

Below: Woolley's antechinus

BRUSH-TAILED PHASCOGALE

(Phascogale tapoatafa)

Phascogales spend their nights foraging up and down tree trunks. Here, they glean a variety of invertebrates from under the bark and out of cracks and hollows. They occasionally take other small animals. Their hind feet can be rotated in any direction, allowing them to climb up or down with equal ease. These tree specialists also have long dexterous toes with sharp claws.

DESCRIPTION: This marsupial is grey and has a distinctive black bushy tail. It has a narrow face, large eyes with blue around the iris and large pointed ears.

OTHER NAMES: Black-tailed phascogale, common wambenger, tuan.

STATUS AND DISTRIBUTION: Phascogales inhabit forest and woodland areas in high-rainfall areas throughout Australia. It is found in northern parts of the Kimberley. The distribution of this marsupial has been significantly reduced because of clearing. It is now considered threatened, having disappeared from several regions, and become much less abundant in others.

PREFERRED HABITAT: They live in woodlands and forests with enough older trees to provide the numerous hollows and food sources that phascogales require.

LIFE HISTORY: Phascogales are solitary and occupy fairly large territories in which they will have many nest sites, which are usually in hollows in the canopy. Large trees with many broken limbs provide the best nest sites. Phascogales only come to the ground to move to another tree. All males die shortly after a frenzy of mating during a well-defined breeding season. This

phenomenon is common in the family of marsupials to which the phascogale belongs (dasyurids) and probably has the purpose of reducing competition for food, so that nursing females and dispersing young have a greater chance of surviving. Females have up to eight young which spend about two months in the pouch and are then deposited in a suitable hollow. Juveniles breed in their first year.

HOW TO SEE THEM: Spotlighting in woodland areas may reveal a phascogale foraging in a tree.

DUNNARTS

(Sminthopsis sp.*)*

Though largely unseen, these small marsupials are numerous throughout most of the Australian bush, from the south-west forests to the deserts. In the arid regions, they have survived where most medium-sized mammals have become locally or totally extinct. At least six species are present in north-western Australia. These include the red-cheeked dunnart (*Sminthopsis virginiae*), Butler's dunnart (*S. butleri*), stripe-faced dunnart (*S. macroura*), hairy-footed dunnart (*S. hirtipes*), lesser hairy-footed dunnart (*S. youngsoni*) and long-tailed dunnart (*S. longicaudata*).

Dunnarts are carnivorous and eat mostly insects and spiders. Small vertebrates such as house mice and lizards are sometimes taken. They have pointed noses, large eyes and proportionally large and rounded ears. Their bodies resemble those of mice. All dunnart species are nocturnal.

The red-cheeked dunnart, which is found in the wetter northern Kimberley, has a thin tail, reddish cheeks and short, spiky fur. It also has an attractive dark stripe down the front of its head. It seems to prefer open savannah woodland. The female builds a saucer-shaped nest lined with leaf fragments and grass in which to keep her litter of eight or so, presumably when they are old enough to leave the pouch.

Butler's dunnart is less well known but is thought to be locally common in many high-rainfall areas of the northern Kimberley. They are brown with grey specks and white undersides, have a darker head stripe and dark ring around the eye. Their hind feet differ slightly from other species of dunnart.

Living in a harsher and more arid climate than the red-cheeked and Butler's dunnarts, stripe-faced dunnarts have fatter tails, which are used to store fat as a source of energy in lean times.

Hairy-footed dunnart

The length of the tail is about 1.25 times that of its body, which distinguishes it from other dunnarts. They are widely distributed throughout arid and semi-arid parts of Australia and shelter by day under rocks and logs. Like other desert specialists, they are well-adapted to take advantage of cyclical deserts conditions of long drought followed by sudden heavy rainfall, and breed quickly to take advantage of good conditions. Gestation only takes 12 days and up to eight young are suckled within the mother's pouch for about 40 days. They are weaned after 70 days.

The hairy footed dunnart, found in the deserts south of the tropics, has relatively long and quite wide feet covered with fine silvery hair. The lesser hairy-footed dunnart is found in the Great Sandy Desert and Exmouth Gulf region.

WHERE TO SEE THEM: These small, nocturnal and secretive creatures are rarely seen.

NINGAUI

(Ningaui sp.*)*

Ningaui will tackle cockroaches and centipedes larger than themelves without fear, often undertaking a titanic struggle to subdue their chosen prey. Small skinks and grasshoppers are probably also eaten. There are two species of ningaui - Pilbara ningaui (*Ningaui timealeyi*) and Wongai ningaui (*Ningaui ridei*).

DESCRIPTION: These tiny marsupials are only half the size of a house mouse with a maximum head and body length of 57 millimetres, and tails up to 79 millimetres long. They weigh between two and 10 grams. The Pilbara ningaui has grey fur while the Wongai ningaui has reddish-brown fur. Unlike planigales and dunnarts, their fur is bristly. The ear has a large outer edge.

STATUS AND DISTRIBUTION: Pilbara ningaui are confined to semi-arid grasslands of the Pilbara. Wongai ningaui occupy the eastern Pilbara and Goldfields and throughout central Australia.

PREFERRED HABITAT: The Pilbara ningaui is found on drainage lines and on plains near ridges and outcrops, which are moister and therefore more densely vegetated while the Wongai prefers arid sandy inland habitats.

LIFE HISTORY: Ningaui hunt by night. By day they shelter in hummocks of spinifex, logs and burrows. Males compete aggressively for females during the breeding season and females with pouch young will not tolerate the presence of other adults.

Each female produces between five to eight young between September and March. By March, most of the adults have disappeared, since ningaui are short-lived and few survive beyond a year.

KULTARR

(Antechinomys laniger)

Superficially resembling a miniature kangaroo, the kultarr has long hind legs, short forelegs and a long thin tail with a distinct dark brown to black brush on the end. However, it bounds along, using both its forelegs and hind legs.

DESCRIPTION: These mouse-sized marsupials have a covering of greyish to sandy brown fur, with a white chest and belly. The face and crown has a darker line and the large eyes are surrounded by a darker eye-ring. Their ears are very large and rounded. Their pencil-thin tails are held in the air. The head and body length of adults is only 85 millimetres long, with a 125 millimetre tail.

OTHER NAMES: Wuhl-wuhl, pitchi-pitchi, Jerboa pouched mouse.

STATUS AND DISTRIBUTION: Though not regarded as threatened, the kultarr is uncommon and has disappeared from parts of its former range. The species is found across most of central arid Australia. Like other animals of the desert, they breed after good rains to take advantage of abundant food.

PREFERRED HABITAT: Kultarrs are arid specialists, inhabiting spinifex plains, stony and sandy country with low vegetation and mulga areas. These marsupials sometimes take over the burrows of large trapdoor spiders or hopping mice.

LIFE HISTORY: The kultarr is nocturnal, spending most of the night hunting insects. A fold of skin develops into a pouch during the breeding season to provide protection for the suckling young. At 30 days old, when they are 25 millimetres long, the young become too big for the pouch and either ride on the mother's back or are left in the nest. They are weaned at three months of age.

WHERE TO SEE THEM: These nocturnal, hopping marsupials are extremely secretive and unlikely to be seen.

PLANIGALES

(Planigale sp.*)*

The long-tailed planigale (*Planigale ingrami*) is the smallest marsupial and one of the smallest mammals in the world. On average, adults weigh little more than four grams and are about six centimetres long. What it lacks in size it more than makes up for in aggression, frequently attacking and killing prey larger than its own body. Grasshoppers and other insects, larvae, small reptiles and the young of other small mammals are eaten. The common planigale (*Planigale maculata*) is also found in north-western Australia. Although the biggest of the four species of planigale, it still only reaches about eight centimetres long and weighs just 10 to 12 grams.

DESCRIPTION: These mouse-sized creatures have very flattened heads with an elongated snout, very large ears and relatively small eyes. The body of the long-tailed planigale is covered with quite long brownish-grey fur. Its thin tail is longer than its head and body, whereas that of the common planigale is shorter.

OTHER NAMES: The long-tailed planigale is also called Ingram's planigale or northern planigale, while the common planigale is also known as the coastal planigale.

STATUS AND DISTRIBUTION: The long-tailed planigale is found through most of the Pilbara and Kimberley, including the Great Sandy Desert, and in parts of the Northern Territory and Queensland. The common planigale is found in the northern Kimberley, the top third of the Northern Territory and down the coasts of Queensland and northern New South Wales.

PREFERRED HABITAT: The long-tailed planigale inhabits tussocks of spinifex, cracks beneath rocks and crevices within cracking soil. The common planigale builds a saucer-shaped nest beneath a rock or log.

LIFE HISTORY: Planigales are nocturnal. Between four and 12 young are born and raised in a well-developed pouch that opens to the rear. At six weeks of age they are placed in a grassy nest beneath fallen bark, leaf litter or a spinifex tussock while the mother goes on hunting forays. The youngsters are weaned and leave home at three months.

WHERE TO SEE THEM: These tiny, secretive animals are unlikely to be seen.

Above: Long-tailed planigale Below: Common planigale

NORTHERN BROWN BANDICOOT

(Isoodon macrourus)

Northern brown bandicoots have the shortest gestation period of any mammal – a mere 12 and a half days. The reproductive capacity of this animal is remarkable. They produce up to seven young, although usually only from two to four survive to weaning, which occurs after 50 days. A new litter is born as soon as the previous one is weaned. As a result, females can give birth to several litters every year. Like many bandicoots, these baby factories become sexually mature even before they are fully grown.

DESCRIPTION: These species are the biggest of the bandicoots, growing up to 400 millimetres long (head and body length) with long tails up to 215 millimetres. They are speckled brownish-black in colour.

OTHER NAMES: Brindled bandicoot, long-tailed short-nosed bandicoot, garimbu.

STATUS AND DISTRIBUTION: They are common in far northern Australia, including most of the Kimberley, and most of the eastern coast.

PREFERRED HABITAT: Northern brown bandicoots live in areas with reasonable ground cover, including grasslands, woodlands and open forest. They are common in gardens of outer urban areas on the east coast as far south as Sydney.

LIFE HISTORY: Northern brown bandicoots feed on insects, spiders, earthworms, berries, grass seeds and more. They inhabit home ranges of between one and six hectares and show aggression to other bandicoots invading their territory. They are nocturnal and shelter by day in nests consisting of a shallow depression covered with litter. Hollow logs and spinifex tussocks also provide refuge.

Photo - Nature Focus Library/H & J Beste

WHERE TO SEE THEM: It may be possible to see them if you go spotlighting near the denser vegetation along creeklines of the far north Kimberley.

GOLDEN BANDICOOT

***(Isoodon* sp.)**

Genetic studies on the golden bandicooot have shown that it is very similar to the southern brown bandicoot and it is likely that the scientific name will change to reflect this. It may therefore become a northern extension of the southern bandicoot, or quenda population. However, due to the isolation of this population and the very different habitat it occupies, different management considerations may be necessary.

DESCRIPTION: As their name suggests, golden bandicoots are clothed in stiff golden black-brown hair, which is sleek and shiny. Smaller than the bandicoots of the south, they have the broad, curved pointed nose and arched back typical of all bandicoots.

OTHER NAMES: Wintaru, nyulu.

STATUS AND DISTRIBUTION: The northern population has declined seriously since European settlement. Formerly considered endangered, they had completely disappeared from the central deserts by the 1950s and are now restricted to Barrow and Middle islands, off the Pilbara coast, and a small part of the far north Kimberley, including Augustus Island. Another population was discovered on an island off Arnhemland in the Northern Territory.

PREFERRED HABITAT: They inhabit spinifex and sand dune areas on Barrow Island and spinifex, low woodlands and the edges of rainforest patches in the Kimberley.

LIFE HISTORY: Golden bandicoots have a varied diet that includes invertebrates, small reptiles and rodents, turtle eggs and plant roots. Nocturnal and usually solitary, they breed year-round and give birth to two or three young. One or two of the young may survive.

WHERE TO SEE THEM: They are commonly seen foraging at night by workers on Barrow Island, but people are unlikely to see them elsewhere because of their nocturnal habits and occurrence in isolated areas. They make small, conical diggings.

BILBY

(Macrotis lagotis)

The bilby has survived where other desert-dwellers have disappeared, and it is one very few medium-sized mammals still found in WA's desert regions. In recent years, there have been calls for this strikingly attractive and uniquely Australian mammal to be promoted in place of the Easter bunny. Bilbies breed well in captivity and are currently being returned to suitable parts of their former range.

DESCRIPTION: The bilby has long rabbit-like ears, a long pointed snout and a long black and white crested tail. They are covered with soft bluish-grey fur. Males may grow twice the size of females.

OTHER NAMES: Dalgyte, rabbit-eared bandicoot, ninu, walpajirri.

STATUS AND DISTRIBUTION: Once distributed throughout arid and semi-arid Australia, the bilby is now confined to northern deserts, including parts of the Pilbara. It is listed as a threatened species.

PREFERRED HABITAT: Bilbies live in open arid country with spinifex grasslands and acacia shrublands.

LIFE HISTORY: Bilbies are largely solitary, widely dispersed and occur in low numbers. They are comparatively slow-moving but have superb hearing. They also have strong claws and are very efficient burrowers. In sandy soil, they can disappear from sight within three minutes. Their burrows go down in a steep spiral to a depth of about two metres. The steep descent makes it very

difficult for predators such as foxes and cats to unearth a bilby. However, they were a favourite food of Aboriginal people. Bilbies dig burrows wherever they go and may use as many as two dozen at any one time. These nocturnal animals always feed close to a burrow, mostly within

100 metres or so, and may visit several burrows each night before choosing one in which to spend the daylight hours. Their main food items are bulbs and insects such as termites, witchetty grubs and honeypot ants. Bilbies have a high breeding rate in good times and can breed throughout the year, an adaptation which allows them to quickly take advantage of good seasons in the harsh desert environment.

WHERE TO SEE THEM: These secretive animals are seen on rare occasions. Desert travellers may be able to locate their burrows and diggings.

ROCK RINGTAIL POSSUM

(Pseudocheirus dahli)

Unlike other possums, rock ringtails prefer to live among rock piles, rather than in trees. As a result, they have shorter tails, legs and claws than other possums. They are secretive and nocturnal and live in areas with large boulders which contain deep fissures. Relatively little is known about them, as they live off the beaten track and are difficult to catch.

DESCRIPTION: Rock ringtails have dense woolly fur and a long, flexible tail used to grasp branches during climbing. The tail has a furry base but is almost bare at the tip. The underside is also devoid of fur for about two-thirds of its length. The fur is reddish-grey and they have a central stripe down their back, from the head to the middle of the back.

OTHER NAMES: Rock possum, wogoit.

STATUS AND DISTRIBUTION: Rock ringtails are thought to be common within their range, although restricted to relatively small areas in the northern Kimberley. Though not considered threatened, they are on the priority fauna list, which means their status requires monitoring and review.

LIFE HISTORY: These animals are vegetarians, feeding on flowers, fruits and leaves. They are quite timid and remain close to their rocky homes when feeding. If caught in a spotlight, they immediately retreat (unlike other possums, which freeze) and may temporarily abandon an area soon afterwards. They breed year round, giving birth to one youngster. Like other possums, the babies are carried on the mother's back once they leave the pouch.

WHERE TO SEE THEM: Rock ringtails are rarely seen, but if you are near rocky outcrops in the north Kimberley look for their distinctive reddish-brown droppings. They look like slightly bent cigars, and may be up to 25 millimetres long. The species is sometimes seen at night on the limestone slopes of the Napier Range, west of Windjana Gorge.

Photo - Nature Focus Library/Ian Morris

Photo - Nature Focus Library/S Swanson

SUGAR GLIDER

(Petaurus breviceps)

The most notable feature of these small attractive mammals is their ability to glide from tree to tree, steering by means of membranes that stretch from finger to toe. They are communal and live in social groups of up to seven adults and their offspring.

DESCRIPTION: These small nocturnal animals have large eyes and delicate pointed faces. The fur on their upper bodies is bluish-grey to brownish-grey. A dark central stripe runs from between the eyes to the centre of the back. The underside is cream to pale grey and the bushy grey or black tail may be tipped with white.

OTHER NAMES: Sugar squirrel, lesser flying phalanger, lesser glider.

STATUS AND DISTRIBUTION: In WA, sugar gliders are found only in the Kimberley, although they extend across the north of Australia, down the east coast to Victoria and have been introduced to Tasmania. They are common throughout their range.

PREFERRED HABITAT: They inhabit forest and woodland areas with suitable tree hollows.

LIFE HISTORY: They feed on the gum exuded by some species of wattle, the sap of some eucalypts, as well as invertebrates, and even peaceful doves. Sugar gliders nest in tree hollows lined with leaves. Hollows are shared with other members of their social group. Each female produces two pouch young. By two months of age they are old enough to be left in the nest and in another month they begin to accompany their mothers on foraging trips. At seven to 10 months they are forced out in search of a new territory and at this time many die. Birds are the main predators.

WHERE TO SEE THEM: Visitors to Mount Hart homestead, 50 kilometres off the Gibb River Road, may see them in the homestead gardens at night.

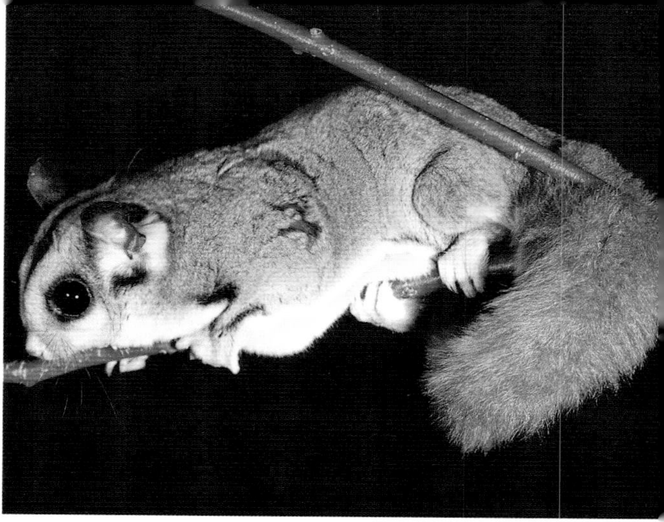

Tracks

Droppings

NORTHERN BRUSHTAIL POSSUM

(Trichosurus vulpecula arnhemensis)

The northern brushtail possum was once considered to be a separate species to the common brushtail possum of southern, central and eastern Australia, but is now classed as a subspecies of the common brushtail. Abundant over much of Australia, brushtails were hunted extensively for their pelts and were a favoured food of Aboriginal people.

DESCRIPTION: Male northern brushtails are usually reddish-grey and the females silvery-grey, but occasionally reddish. Both sexes have a pale belly. Unlike that of the southern form, the tail has little fur and the underside is naked. Brushtail possums have large eyes, erect, prominent ears and pointed faces. Females weigh 1.3 kilograms and males 1.6 kilograms.

STATUS AND DISTRIBUTION: Northern brushtail possums are uncommon in the Pilbara with only three mainland populations known from the region. However, they are common on Barrow Island. They are found across most of the Kimberley and in the northern half of the Northern Territory. Throughout their range, they are common in areas of suitable woodland, though their overall distribution is patchy. However, they have disappeared from large areas in more arid country.

PREFERRED HABITAT: They live in open forest and woodland wherever there are sufficient older trees to provide hollows. They may also shelter in crevices within rocky areas such as breakaways and mesa slopes. They inhabit roofs in Darwin.

LIFE HISTORY: At night, brushtails will spend some time on the ground moving from tree to tree in search of the fresh growth on young trees. The eat leaves, fruits and blossoms. Hollows in

Photo - Jiri Lochman

larger old and dead trees are used for daytime refuge. On Barrow Island in the Pilbara, where there are no trees, the possums have a shorter tail and nest in termite mounds, limestone caves and boodie warrens. Northern brushtails breed year round. Brushtails only have one young, but most survive until weaned at five or six months. They are quite territorial, with the males scent-marking and defending their one-hectare home range.

HOW TO SEE THEM: A spotlighting excursion in areas of suitable woodland may be rewarded with a sighting. Using a small boat and a spotlight at high tide, you can find them during August and September, feeding in mangroves on the seaward fringe of the stand that extends south from Walsh Point, north of Mitchell Plateau.

SCALY-TAILED POSSUM

(Wyulda squamicauldata)

This fascinating and little-known species looks like a cross between a brushtail possum and a cuscus and shares some characteristics of both. Like cuscuses, its tail is naked and prehensile. About a fifth of its tail is furred and the rest is scaly.

DESCRIPTION: The scaly-tailed possum is rabbit-sized. Most of its fur is pale grey in colour but a darker stripe extends down the centre of its back, from the shoulders to the rump. The fur on the base of the tail is quite reddish. It also has creamy white underparts, large, bulging brown eyes and rounded ears.

OTHER NAMES: The Worara people call it ilangnalya.

STATUS AND DISTRIBUTION: It may be common in limited areas such as Boongaree Island and Kalumburu, in the far north Kimberley, but is on the priority fauna list because relatively little is known about the status of the species.

PREFERRED HABITAT: The scaly-tailed possum inhabits rugged rocky country in high rainfall parts of the Kimberley.

LIFE HISTORY: During the day this mammal shelters deep in rock piles, emerging at night to feed in trees. Blossoms appear to be the staple diet in the wild, but it may also feed on fruits, nuts, leaves and insects. Females give birth to a single young during the dry season. Little else is known about the species.

WHERE TO SEE THEM: Visitors to Kalumburu may see a scaly-tailed possum if they go spotlighting at night.

BOODIE

(Bettongia lesueur)

The boodie is the only member of the kangaroo family that regularly inhabits burrows. This attractive mammal species went from being exceptionally abundant and widespread to becoming completely extinct on the Australian mainland. It is now confined to four islands off the coast of WA – Barrow and Boodie islands in the Pilbara and Bernier and Dorre islands off Carnarvon. The main culprit in its disappearance is thought to be the introduced fox. Old boodie warrens can still be seen in the arid zone, where some have been taken over by rabbits and goannas.

DESCRIPTION: These 'rat kangaroos' vary considerably in size. Those on Barrow Island are noticeably smaller than those on Bernier and Dorre islands. They are grey, thickset and rounded, with a hunched posture. Their ears are rounded and their tail is quite stout.

OTHER NAMES: Burrowing bettong, Lesueur's rat kangaroo, burrowing rat kangaroo.

STATUS AND DISTRIBUTION: Boodies are regarded as endangered, because of the low number of populations. However, they are common on fox-free Barrow Island. They were once found across most of southern Australia and north to Broome. Populations have recently been established at Shark Bay – on the mainland at Heirrisson Prong in an area which was fenced off and baited for feral animals – and on Faure Island after the removal of feral cats.

PREFERRED HABITAT: These mammals inhabit spinifex grasslands. They prefer areas with easily excavated loamy soils and often make their burrow systems underneath limestone caprock.

LIFE HISTORY: Boodies are highly social, living in complex warrens with numerous entrances and interconnecting passages. A warren on Barrow Island, for instance, has 120 entrances and at least 60 inhabitants. Within the warrens are numerous nests padded with grasses. Boodies eat roots, bulbs, fungi, seeds, nuts, termites and fruit, foraging entirely at night. They smell out the food source and then usually dig it out. They have a short gestation period and, though they only produce a single joey at a time, they may raise three young in a year.

SPECTACLED HARE-WALLABY

(Lagorchestes conspicillatus)

The bright orange rings around its eyes give the spectacled hare-wallaby its name and make it easily distinguished from other hare-wallabies. This medium-sized mammal is a desert specialist which never drinks. It obtains all the moisture it needs from the vegetation it grazes. It prefers to eat tender colonising shrubs but in long unburnt or undisturbed areas the tips of spinifex leaves form a large part of this animal's diet.

OTHER NAMES: Wurkalpi, yulkaminyi, milpatiri, wampana.

DESCRIPTION: These wallabies are about a metre long, with the long tail comprising about half this length. They have fluffy brown fur which is white at the tip. The feet are lighter in colour and the undersides are white. These robust animals are quite thick set, with a short neck. The tail is grey-brown, has shorter hair and may be darker near the tip.

STATUS AND DISTRIBUTION: Spectacled hare-wallabies are rare and regarded as threatened in WA, although they are abundant on Barrow Island, off the Pilbara coast. Feral cats are believed to be responsible for the extinction of a population on the Montebello Islands, so these predators are also likely to be a factor in their decline on the mainland. They occur only in scattered populations in the Kimberley.

LIFE HISTORY: During the day, these nocturnal animals keep cool by sheltering in hides they have tunnelled in spinifex hummocks. They are usually solitary animals but up to three may be seen feeding together. They breed throughout the year but on Barrow Island births peak in March and September. The single young leave their mothers' pouches after about 150 days. Females mature at about one year of age.

WHERE TO SEE THEM: They might be seen at night in some areas of the Pilbara, such as the road into Shay Gap, and along the Gibb River Road in the Kimberley. They are often sighted on Barrow Island.

NORTHERN NAILTAIL WALLABY

(Onchogalea unguifera)

Unlike its extinct cousin, the crescent nailtail wallaby, the northern nailtail has survived European settlement and is still quite common in some parts of northern Australia.

DESCRIPTION: This small sandy-coloured wallaby has a tuft of dark hairs towards the end of its tail and a distinct protrusion or 'nail' on the tip. A dark stripe runs along the centre of its back from the lower back to the tail. Males have a combined head and body length of about 600 millimetres. Females are slightly smaller.

OTHER NAMES: Karrabul, sandy nailtail, wutu-wutu.

STATUS AND DISTRIBUTION: They are found across most of the Kimberley and northern parts of the Northern Territory and Queensland. Within this range, their distribution is patchy, and the species has probably declined since European settlement.

PREFERRED HABITAT: Northern nailtail wallabies inhabit lightly wooded floodplains, open grassy woodlands and shrubby savannah grasslands. They are more common along watercourses.

LIFE HISTORY: The northern nailtail wallaby tends to be solitary but may feed in groups of up to four. It is nocturnal. Little is known of its biology.

WHERE TO SEE THEM: They are found at the Bungle Bungle Range in Purnululu National Park but are unlikely to be seen because of their nocturnal habits. They can often be seen in headlights if you are driving along roads and tracks of the Dampier Peninsula, north of Broome, at night.

ROCK-WALLABIES

Rock-wallabies are sometimes flushed from their hiding places during the day but the usual view is of their backsides, as they bound towards the nearest rocky cover. People who have traversed rocky slopes inhabited by these mammals can attest to their impressive speed. Five of the 15 recognised species of rock-wallaby inhabit north-western Australia: the short-eared rock-wallaby (*Petrogale brachyotis*), the monjon (*P. burbidgei*), the nabarlek or little rock-wallaby (*P. concinnus*), Rothschild's rock-wallaby (*P. rothschildi*) and the black-footed rock-wallaby (*P. lateralis*). These small marsupials are extremely attractive and often have interesting markings. Their hind feet are thick and padded and resemble the radial tyres of cars - this is good for moving around their rocky habitat.

DESCRIPTION: Short-eared rock wallabies have short fur and ears. The back is light grey and there is a dark brown neck stripe from behind the ears to the shoulder. The undersides are white to greyish-white and the tail is darker at the end. The monjon is the smallest of the rock-wallabies. Its back is olive-coloured but marbled with black and fawn. The orange face features a light stripe from the eye to the ear. The tail is a light greyish-olive, the flanks a deep olive and the undersides yellowish. The species has shorter ears than the nabarlek (less than 35 millimetres long). The nabarlek is a dull reddish-colour with light grey and black marbling and greyish-white beneath. The tail is tipped with a black brush and a dark but indistinct shoulder stripe can sometimes be seen. Rothschild's rock-wallabies have dark brown ears and upper faces, while the neck, throat and cheeks are a very light grey. The rest of the body is greyish-brown above and light brown below,

Opposite: Black-footed rock-wallaby

with a darker tail. However, the back of the neck and shoulders can sometimes be a purplish colour. Black-footed rock-wallabies are generally greyish-brown, with some grey on their head and shoulders. The brownish-grey tail ends in a black brush. They have a whitish and dark brown side stripe. They have a light stripe on the cheek and a dark stripe from the forehead to the mid-back.

STATUS AND DISTRIBUTION: Short-eared rock-wallabies are found across most of the Kimberley (other than the deserts) and northern parts of the Northern Territory. Relatively little is known about the status of the monjou as it is confined to rugged parts of the far north Kimberley. The nabarlek is found over a wider area of the northern Kimberley and far north Northern Territory. Rothschild's rock-wallabies are reasonably common and found in the Hamersley Range and Chichester Range and the Dampier Archipelago, near Karratha, in the Pilbara. Black-footed rock-wallabies are regarded as threatened and those in the Kimberley are confined to a very small area in the south of the region.

PREFERRED HABITAT: Rocky hills, cliffs and gorges.

LIFE HISTORY: Rock-wallabies mostly eat grass but they may also browse on herbs, leaves and fruit. They are most active at night but may feed in the late afternoon and bask during the early morning. Breeding is fairly continuous after the female reaches sexual maturity. After they have left the pouch, the young are usually deposited in a sheltered position while the mother goes foraging. She regularly returns to suckle them until they are weaned. In other parts of Australia, including the Pilbara region, foxes have considerably reduced rock-wallaby populations. Fortunately, foxes cannot tolerate the high temperatures and high humidity in the Kimberley, so rock-wallabies are reasonably secure in the region.

Rothschild's rock-wallaby

WHERE TO SEE THEM: Many reasonably-sized rocky outcrops in the Pilbara and Kimberley harbour rock-wallabies. Visitors to Yardie Creek, in Cape Range National Park south of Exmouth, are likely to see black-footed rock-wallabies along the gorge walls. In the Pilbara, populations of Rothschild's rock-wallabies are found on Dolphin, Enderby, Rosemary and West Lewis islands and in Karijini National Park, Millstream-Chichester National Park and the Burrup Peninsula. The black-footed rock-wallaby thrives on Barrow Island, an important nature reserve off the Pilbara coast.

AGILE WALLABY

(Macropus agilis)

The agile wallaby is the most commonly seen mammal of the Kimberley. They are numerous, relatively large and active by day. These nervous animals are often startled by passing vehicles, their bodies remaining quite upright as they hop rapidly away.

DESCRIPTION: Males average 800 millimetres in length and are larger than females, which average 650 millimetres. They are sandy brown in colour with white undersides. They may have a dark brown stripe in the centre of their head between the eyes and ears, and a faint buff-coloured cheek stripe. The thigh also has a light stripe.

OTHER NAMES: Kimberley wallaby, sandy wallaby, grass wallaby, river wallaby.

STATUS AND DISTRIBUTION: Agile wallabies are common throughout tropical areas of northern Australia that lie within reasonable distance of the coast.

PREFERRED HABITAT: This species inhabits areas of open forest and grasslands adjacent to streams.

LIFE HISTORY: Like some kangaroos, agile wallabies appear to have benefited from European settlement because of increased pasture and additional water points. They are attracted to areas regenerating after fire, which have an abundance of tender young

herbs and grasses. They eat most native grasses and may dig into the soil to obtain the roots of ribbon grass. Native fruits, such as figs, and coolabah leaves are also consumed. Breeding can occur year round. The joey stays in the pouch for seven to eight months and is weaned between 10 to 12 months. Agile wallabies mate

soon after birth but the embryo remains dormant. As a result, the new young begins to develop as soon as the joey leaves the pouch.

WHERE TO SEE THEM: Watch for them in riverine vegetation and nearby grasslands throughout the Kimberley.

Tracks

EURO

(Macropus robustus)

The euro is found throughout the Kimberley, the Great Sandy Desert and Pilbara. If they have sufficient shelter from the sun and food plants containing reasonable moisture, these desert specialists can survive for long periods without drinking.

DESCRIPTION: This small kangaroo or wallaroo has dark grey to reddish fur on its back and head, with lighter grey fur below. The end of the muzzle is bare and black. Adults measure from a little over a metre long, from nose to tail tip, to almost two metres in larger males. Mature males may weigh twice as much as females and are usually darker (except for euros on Barrow Island, where both sexes are the same size).

OTHER NAMES: Common wallaroo.

STATUS AND DISTRIBUTION: These mammals are common and distributed across most of the Australian continent. The northern subspecies is restricted to the Kimberley and the Northern Territory. There is a smaller distinct subspecies on Barrow Island.

PREFERRED HABITAT: Euros tend to shelter in caves, overhanging rocks and ledges within steep escarpments, rocky hills or stony rises and graze in the lower slopes and surrounding plains.

LIFE HISTORY: These kangaroos tend to be solitary. They feed on grasses and shrubs. Like other kangaroos, euros carrying joeys have a dormant embryo in their womb, ready to resume development when the pouch is vacated.

WHERE TO SEE THEM: Euros are common along the Great Northern Highway between Broome and Turkey Creek, especially in the early morning and late afternoon. They can also be seen at Cape Range National Park.

Droppings

ANTILOPINE WALLAROO

(Macropus antilopinus)

This large kangaroo was named *antilopinus* because its long, fine fur is supposed to be similar to that of an antelope. Its appearance is quite similar to grey and red kangaroos.

DESCRIPTION: Males have reddish-tan backs and paler limbs and underparts. However, their paws and hind feet are tipped with black. On average, their total length is close to two metres. The females usually have a pale grey head. The rest of their body is either grey throughout or a similar colouring to the males. Females are also considerably smaller than males, with an average length of one a half metres including the tail.

OTHER NAMES: Antelope kangaroo.

STATUS AND DISTRIBUTION: Antilopine wallaroos are found in the northern Kimberley, northern parts of the Northern Territory and northern Queensland. They are reasonably common.

PREFERRED HABITAT: Open, tropical woodland areas with a grassy understorey. They are usually seen in flat or gently sloping areas.

LIFE HISTORY: Antilopine wallaroos are social animals. Although they are usually seen in pairs or alone, they are thought to live in groups of three to eight. Larger groups of 30 or more sometimes form. Their activity is determined by the weather. At hotter times they will rest in shady areas during the day, but if it is overcast and rainy they will graze at any time of the day. Few studies have been done on this animal, but it is believed that birth takes place year-round, with most young born in the late wet or early dry season.

Photo - Nature Focus Library/LF & OG Schick

RED KANGAROO

(Macropus rufus)

Not all 'red' kangaroos are red. Many females, known as blue fliers, are bluish-grey. Most males are red but the occasional bluish-grey male is sometimes found. The red kangaroo is one of the largest living marsupials. Majestic, old, scarred males can reach almost two and a half metres long, including the metre-long tails. They can weigh up to 85 kilograms and live up to 20 years.

DESCRIPTION: Adults differ from other kangaroos in having distinctly white underparts, a black and white patch on each side of the muzzle and a white stripe from the mouth to the ear.

OTHER NAMES: Marloo, plains kangaroo.

STATUS AND DISTRIBUTION: Red kangaroos are abundant and found through most of the Australian mainland. In WA they are absent only from the Kimberley and the south-west corner.

PREFERRED HABITAT: Grasslands with scattered trees, mulga and mallee areas, deserts and shrublands.

LIFE HISTORY: Red kangaroos usually live in 'mobs' consisting of a dominant male, several sexually mature females and their young. Red kangaroos are nomadic and will move into areas of recent good rains, where young grasses and herbs have sprung from the ground. Breeding may be suppressed if environmental conditions are unfavourable. The hairless newborn weighs less than a gram and immediately moves to the pouch and attaches itself to one of the four teats. There it remains for about eight months. When it leaves the pouch, a dormant embryo that has been carried by the mother immediately begins to develop and is born soon afterwards. Remarkably, the mother is able to produce milk of varying chemical consistencies for the pouch young and the older joey, which continues to suckle.

WHERE TO SEE THEM: Anyone travelling along the Great Northern Highway is bound to see groups of red kangaroos, especially if it is early or late in the day. Take care to avoid hitting them.

BLACK FLYING FOX

(Pteropus alecto)

These flying mammals are often first located by their incessant chatter and their pungent smell. At Geikie Gorge, the freshwater crocodiles that also inhabit the gorge sometimes leap from the water to snaffle the odd bat.

DESCRIPTION: This is the largest species of flying fox. It can grow up to 260 millimetres long and attain a wingspan of a metre or more. There is a reddish collar around the back of the neck and their eyes may also have brown rings. Short black fur covers the entire body and their face resembles that of a very small dog or fox, hence its common name.

OTHER NAMES: Gould's fruit-bat, black fruit bat.

STATUS AND DISTRIBUTION: Black flying foxes are common in all coastal and near coastal areas of northern Australia, where they form large colonies made up of tens of thousands of individuals.

PREFERRED HABITAT: Flying foxes inhabit the mangroves, paperbark swamps and rainforest patches that are associated with most northern rivers. They particularly favour mangrove islands found in the estuaries of major rivers.

LIFE HISTORY: Each evening flying foxes set off from their roosting colonies at the same time. Those who are lucky enough to be in the right spot at the right time may witness an exodus of thousands of bats heading towards their nightly feeding grounds. They may travel up to 50 kilometres from their base to find and feed on eucalypt, paperbark and turpentine blossoms. They prefer to roost high in the canopy. Older males usually maintain a watch and raise the alarm if intruders appear. During the breeding

Photo - Hans and Judy Beste/Lochman Transparencies

season males establish small territories (circles a metre wide) and proudly display their sexual organs. The young are born in October. They cannot fly and have to be carried by their mothers for the first month, suckling the teats which are near the point where the wing is joined to the body.

WHERE TO SEE THEM: Geikie Gorge National Park in the Kimberley, Millstream-Chichester National Park and occasionally around Karratha, in the Pilbara.

OTHER BATS

Bats are everywhere. Bat-conscious observers can discern their dark bodies in the night sky. More than 30 species of bats are found in northern Australia. One of the most widespread is the yellow-bellied sheath-tailed bat (*Saccalaimus flaviventris*). Its almost metallic tik-tik-tik at half-second intervals may be heard at night, even in large towns. They forage over trees and roof tops and travel very fast, covering huge distances in their nightly feeding forays.

Sometimes smaller, more agile bats can be seen dodging and twisting between trees and bushes in pursuit of insects. Their dexterity is worth watching, especially when you realise that they are emitting sound pulses well beyond the range that we can hear, and listening for echoes to locate obstacles and food.

One noteworthy species is the ghost bat (*Macroderma gigas*), the only Australian member of a family commonly called false vampire bats. These voracious carnivores weigh a hefty 150 grams and feed largely on birds, other bats, mice and small marsupials.

Northern blossom-bats (*Macroglossus minimus*) feed largely on nectar and pollen and play an important role in pollinating some species such as paperbarks. They are small, about 15 grams, and have long muzzles and very long tongues that absorb nectar like a sponge absorbs liquid.

Other northern Australian bats include the little red flying fox (*Pteropus scapulatus*), common sheathtail-bat (*Taphozous georgianus*), Hill's sheathtail-bat (*T. hilli*), northern mastiff-bat (*Chaerophon jobensis*), North Queensland long-eared bat

Opposite: Ghost bat

(*Nyctophilus bifax*), Arnhem Land long-eared bat (*N. arnhemensis*), pygmy long-eared bat (*N. walkeri*), common bent-wing bat (*Miniopterus schreibersii*), Gould's wattled bat (*Chalinolobus gouldii*), hoary bat (*C. nigrogriseus*), large-footed mouse-eared bat (*Myotis adversus*), little broad-nosed bat (*Scotorepens greyii*), western broad-nosed bat (*S. balstoni*), mangrove pipistrelle (*Pipistrellus westralis*), litte cave eptesicus (*Vespadelus cearinus*) and yellow-lipped eptesicus (*V. douglasorum*).

Some tropical bat species roost solely in caves and old mines, such as ghost bats, dusky horseshoe bats (*Hipposideros gilberti*), lesser wart-nosed horseshoe-bats (*H. stenotis*) and orange horseshoe-bats (*Rhinonicteris aurantius*). The horseshoe bats use very high frequency echolocation that allows very high resolution but is only effective at ranges of a metre or two. Others, such as the northern mastiff-bat, roost by day in trees. Many of them will live in small colonies in hollow tree limbs. Some, such as lesser long-eared bats (*Nyctophilus geoffroyi*), live fairly solitary lives under peeling bark, or even in dense clusters of leaves. Sometimes they roost in the dark corners of buildings.

WHERE TO SEE THEM: Some species can be seen roosting in caves, such as those in Tunnel Creek National Park in the Kimberley. Common sheath-tailed bats can readily be viewed in rock crevices at the entrance to Windjana Gorge during the daytime. At night, mangrove areas are productive feeding areas for at least 15 species of bats. On warm, moonless nights, large numbers can be seen taking moths in the street lights of northern towns, or flying over pools along watercourses.

Opposite: Yellow-bellied sheeth-tailed bat

TREE RATS

Tree rats are among our most little-known native animals. They spend much of their time effortlessly scurrying along tree branches and outer foliage in search of food and shelter. Three species of tree-rat inhabit the tropical areas of the north-west Kimberley.

The black-footed tree-rat or djintamoonga (*Mesembriomys gouldii*) is the largest of these, weighing up to 800 grams. It is about the size of a small rabbit, with strength to match. Its coarse grey-black body fur gives it a grizzled look. The golden-backed tree-rat or koorrawal (*M. macrurus*) is more delicate and handsome. It has brown body fur suffused with gold along the head, shoulders and back, and is white underneath. It is about the size of the common pet brown rat, weighing about 300 grams. The smallest species, the brush-tailed tree-rat or pakooma (*Conilurus penicillatus*), only weighs about 180 grams as an adult. Its body fur is grey to golden-brown, with a reddish patch on the neck, and white to cream underneath, often with a grey T-shaped marking on the chest.

Early settlers in the north called these animals "rabbit-rats" because their prominent ears gave them a rabbit-like appearance. Their long, hairy tails end with a white tip in the two larger species, and a distinctive black or white brush in the smaller species. They use their tails for balance when climbing, and often hold them high when bounding along the ground.

These species occupy very different habitats, although their general distribution overlaps. Black-footed tree-rats inhabit tall, open eucalypt forest of woollybutt and stringybark, particularly where there is a relatively dense understorey of small trees or shrubs (such as fan palms and

Brush-tailed tree-rat

pandanus). The golden-backed species, however, prefers rainforest patches and rocky sandstone slopes, sometimes venturing into the adjacent open woodlands. The brush-tailed are most common in open woodlands with a sparse shrub layer and a cover of tall grass such as sorghum. All three species shelter in gum tree hollows, or in the tops of fan palms, or occasionally in buildings.

Tree rats eat seeds, fruits and flowers, but also take termites and some other invertebrates. Black-footed tree-rats also eat pandanus nuts and the hard fruits of some plants such as the wingnut tree.

All three species seem to have declined in abundance since European settlement, with their ranges contracting to the north. Both the black–footed and golden–backed tree rats are listed as priority species in need of further study and protection. Their decline may have been caused by the grazing of introduced cattle and changes in fire regimes, compounded by the patchy and unreliable nature of food resources in the drier inland areas.

WESTERN PEBBLE-MOUND MOUSE

(Pseudomys chapmani)

Can you imagine a small rodent building a home from large piles of stones? Strangely enough, the pebble-mound mouse does exactly that. Averaging only 10 grams in body weight, they are adept at carrying pebbles weighing five grams in their mouths. They push them into position with their front paws. Pebble mound mice are now found only in the Pilbara and Ashburton regions of WA.

DESCRIPTION: They average 60 millimetres long, with tails of about 75 millimetres. They are buff-brown with blacker heads. The throat and undersides are white.

OTHER NAMES: Ngadji.

STATUS AND DISTRIBUTION: Pebble mound mice are on a priority list and are no longer regarded as threatened as they are now known from several places throughout the Pilbara. Abandoned pebble mounds have also been found in the Gascoyne, Murchison and Pilbara coast.

PREFERRED HABITAT: They seem to prefer spinifex grasslands with abundant pebbles. They usually build their mounds on the slopes of hills.

LIFE HISTORY: The mounds range in size between half a square metre to a remarkable nine square metres. The tunnels beneath are U-shaped and connected to entry holes. Like most native rodents, they can give birth to four babies, and appear to be quite social, with up to 15 individuals occupying a single mound. They also move over quite large areas, up to 10 hectares.

WHERE TO SEE THEM: You are unlikely to see a mouse but their mounds can be seen at Karijini National Park. The rangers should be able to tell you where to look. Old mounds are visible behind the Karratha townsite and at Millstream.

OTHER NATIVE RODENTS

Eleven other native rodents are found in north-western Australia. They make up a large proportion of our fauna and are found in every type of habitat.

The carnivorous water-rat or rakali (*Hydromys chrysogaster*) is well-adapted to aquatic life, with a sleek body, waterproof fur, webbed feet and nostrils high on its head. It lives around lakes, streams, rivers and in the north is sometimes found along the coast and around islands. Its presence can be detected by its feeding platforms. These take the form of a flat rock or fallen trunk and contain leftover scraps from meals – parts of crustaceans, large aquatic insects, mussels, birds and fish.

The grassland melomys or loolong (*Melomys burtoni*) has scales that lie side by side like mosaic tiles. They do not overlap like those on the tails of other rodents. This rat is thickset, with short limbs and broad hind feet and is adept at climbing. The common rock-rat or djoorri (*Zyzomys argurus*) and large rock-rat or djookooropa (*Z. woodwardi*) are found only in northern Australia and have unusually thick tails. The rock-rat is smaller, more widely distributed and has a less hairy tail than its relative.

The western chestnut mouse or moolpoo (*Pseudomys nanus*), delicate mouse or molinipi (*P. delicatulus*), sandy inland mouse or mingkiri (*P. hermannsburgensis*) and the Lakeland Downs mouse or kerakenga (*Leggadina lakedownensis*) can be difficult to tell apart. The chestnut mouse is approximately 100 millimetres long with a tail that is a similar length and its grizzled fur is a rich chestnut colour. It has a characteristic paler ring around each eye and is found on some Pilbara islands and in the Kimberley and Northern Territory. The delicate mouse is found in the same areas of the Kimberley but is a lighter colour and considerably smaller. It extends as far south as the Pilbara in near-coastal areas. The sandy

Above: Water-rat

Below: Grassland melomys

inland mouse is found in the Pilbara and more arid inland areas but does not reach the Kimberley. It resembles a house mouse. The Lakeland Downs mouse has a shorter tail, only 60 to 70 per cent of its body length of 90 millimetres. It is grey brown above and lighter below and is found across most of the Kimberley and Pilbara. The spinifex hopping-house or tarrkawarra (*Notomys alexis*) is found in sandy parts of the Pilbara and throughout deserts such as the Great Sandy Desert. It is easily distinguished from other north-western rodents by the large hind legs on which it hops through the spinifex. Its tufted tail is longer than its body.

The long-haired rat or mayaroo (*Rattus villosissimus*), lives in small scattered populations of the Kimberley and central inland Australia. It is sometimes called the plague rat because of its ability to increase in remarkable numbers after periods of good rainfall. It is light grey and grows up to 220 millimetres long (males average 187 millimetres and females 167 millimetres). Tunney's rat or djini (*Rattus tunneyi*) is usually smaller with an average length of 147 millimetres and yellow brown to brown fur. Its tail is shorter than its head and body. It lives in burrows on several Pilbara islands, including two in the Exmouth Gulf, and is widespread in the Kimberley, where it seems to prefer tall grassland near watercourses. The species appears to have become extinct in the south-western Kimberley and in central Australia.

HOW TO SEE THEM: These secretive nocturnal animals are rarely seen. If your house is near unspoilt bushland, it is possible they could be killed and brought in by a cat.

Tracks

DINGO

(Canis familiaris dingo)

Dingoes were the only dog species found on mainland Australia at the time of European settlement, although they are thought to have been introduced by Asian seafarers as recently as 4,000 years ago. Their arrival probably caused the extinction on the mainland of the thylacine and Tasmanian devil. Aboriginal people learnt to use them to hunt animals such as kangaroos, wallabies and possums. Following European settlement, the dingo was regarded as a sheep-killer and was systematically exterminated from many agricultural areas. Interbreeding with domestic dog species also threatens the purity of the race in many areas.

DESCRIPTION: These well-proportioned ginger-coloured dogs usually have white-tipped ears and tails. However, they are occasionally black with tan points. The ears are pointed and the tail is bushy. They may grow almost a metre long and females are smaller than males.

OTHER NAMES: Warrigal, wild dog.

STATUS AND DISTRIBUTION: Dingoes are not threatened but they are by no means as widespread as in the past, especially as they have been poisoned extensively in agricultural areas. Their range once extended throughout the entire Australian mainland. It is likely that dingoes are capable of reducing fox numbers through predation.

PREFERRED HABITAT: In arid areas dingoes are sparsely distributed and relative density varies according to the availability of drinking water and prey.

LIFE HISTORY: Dingoes may hunt live prey or scavenge dead animals. In arid areas they usually eat rodents and rabbits, but in other parts kangaroos and wallabies form the bulk of their

Droppings

diet. They may form packs which hunt co-operatively, enabling them to catch larger prey than they could catch on their own. The social organisation of these packs is similar to that observed in wolves. Reptiles and birds are also eaten. Dingoes had a long association with Aboriginal people, and the species has also been domesticated by other Australians. They breed once a year, giving birth to an average of five pups which are hidden in dens. They communicate with other dingoes by howling.

WHERE TO SEE THEM: Sightings of dingoes in the wild are opportunistic. However, they are active during the day, usually early morning or late afternoon. In the desert they may scavenge around regular camping areas.

SIGHTING RECORD

SPECIES	DATE	LOCALITY
echidna		
northern quoll		
mulgara		
antechinuses	14/5/18	ILUKA
brush-tailed phascogale		
dunnarts		
ningaui		
kultarr		
planigales		
northern brown bandicoot		
golden bandicoot**		
bilby*		
rock ringtail possum*		
sugar glider		
northern brushtail possum		

Above: Northern quoll

SIGHTING RECORD

SPECIES	DATE	LOCALITY
scaly-tailed possum*		
boodie**		
spectacled hare-wallaby*		
northern nailtail wallaby		
rock-wallabies*		
agile wallaby		
euro		
antilopine wallaroo		
red kangaroo		
black flying fox		
bats		
tree rats*		
pebble-mound mouse*		
other native rodents		
dingo		

*If you should see live or dead animals please advise the Department of Environment and Conservation's (DEC's) Wildlife Research Centre on (08) 9405 5100.

** Contact DEC if seen on the mainland.

INDEX

agile wallaby 46-47
antechinuses 10-11
antilopine wallaroo 50-51
bandicoots 22-25
bats 56-59
bilby 26-27
black flying fox 54-55
black-footed rock-wallaby 42-43
black-footed tree-rat 60-61
boodie 36-37
brush-tailed phascogale 12-13
brush-tailed tree-rat 60-61
burrowing bettong 36-37
Butler's dunnart 14-15
planigale 20-21
dalgyte 26-27
dingo 68-69
dunnarts 14-15
echidna 4-5
euro 48-49
fruit bat 54-55
flying foxes 54-57
golden-backed tree-rat 60-61
golden bandicoot 24-25
hairy-footed dunnart 14-15
hare-wallaby 38-39
kangaroos 36-53
kultarr 18-19
lesser hairy-footed dunnart 14-15
little rock-wallaby 42-43
long-tailed dunnart 14-15
long-tailed planigale 20-21
mice 64-67
monjon 42-43
mulgara 8-9
nailtail wallaby 40-41
native rodents 64-65
ningaui 16-17
northern brown bandicoot 22-23
northern brushtail possum 32-33
northern nailtail wallaby 40-41
northern quoll 6-7
pebble mound mouse 62-63
phascogale 12-13
Pilbara ningaui 16-17
planigales 20-21
possums 28-35
quoll 6-7
red-cheeked dunnart 14-15
red kangaroo 52-53
rock ringtail possum 28-29
rock-wallabies 42-45
Rothschild's rock-wallaby 42-43
scaly-tailed possum 34-35
short-eared rock-wallaby 42-43
spectacled hare-wallaby 38-39
stripe-faced dunnart 14-15
sugar glider 30-31
tree rats 60-61
water-rat 64-65
western pebble-mound mouse 52-53
wongai ningaui 16-17

2008330-0509-5000